ASKING QUESTIONS ABOUT POLITICAL CAMPAIGNS

NANCY E. WEISS

Published in the United States of America by Cherry Lake Publishing
Ann Arbor, Michigan
www.cherrylakepublishing.com

Consultants: Barb Palser, Digital Media Executive; Marla Conn, ReadAbility, Inc.
Editorial direction and book production: Red Line Editorial
Book design: Sleeping Bear Press

Photo Credits: Sean Locke/Shutterstock Images, cover, 1; Shutterstock Images, 5, 9, 19, 26; iStockphoto, 6, 13, 14, 22, 25; AP Images, 10, 16; Democratic National Committee/AP Images, 20; Peter Turnley/Corbis, 28

Library of Congress Cataloging-in-Publication Data

Weiss, Nancy E.
  Asking questions about political campaigns / by Nancy E. Weiss.
     pages cm. -- (Asking questions about media)
  Includes bibliographical references and index.
  ISBN 978-1-63362-490-0 (hardcover : alk. paper) -- ISBN 978-1-63362-506-8 (pbk. : alk. paper) -- ISBN 978-1-63362-522-8 (pdf ebook) -- ISBN 978-1-63362-538-9 (hosted ebook)
  1. Political campaigns--United States--Juvenile literature. 2. Campaign management--United States--Juvenile literature.
I. Title.

  JK2281.W45 2015
  324.70973--dc23

                              2015005524

Cherry Lake Publishing would like to acknowledge the work of
the Partnership for 21st Century Skills. Please visit www.p21.org
for more information.

Printed in the United States of America
Corporate Graphics Inc.

ABOUT THE AUTHOR

Nancy E. Weiss is a curriculum and training development consultant for schools, companies, and nonprofits. She loves dogs and is the author of the children's short story "The Vinehurst Dog Escape." She lives in Minneapolis, Minnesota, with her family and her lovely mutt, Josie.

TABLE OF CONTENTS

CHAPTER 1

ELECTION SEASON

You turn on the television for your favorite weeknight show. There they are again: the same two ads for the governor's race that you've seen for the last ten nights.

Uh oh—your parents are at it again. Mom wants the Democratic governor to stay in office. Dad wants change. He argues that the Republican **candidate** will create more jobs. You scratch your head and wonder: Whom would I choose?

The next day, you ride your bike to school. In your neighborhood you see signs on lawns and in store windows. The bright, bold signs feature the names of your mom's and dad's choices. You see signs for candidates from other parties too. There's even a billboard funded by a community group hoping to raise

Political campaigns are hard to avoid, even when you're watching your favorite TV shows.

Campaign signs pop up on lawns in all types of neighborhoods during election season.

taxes for schools. Just down the street is another billboard asking you to vote the opposite way.

During an election, campaign messages are everywhere. It seems as if everyone wants a different candidate. People feel so strongly about all kinds of issues—roads and bridges, schools, taxes, and jobs. You ask yourself, "How will I decide how to vote when I turn 18? How will I know what's important to me?"

To be an informed citizen, it's important to learn more about political campaigns. In particular, you should be able to answer the following questions:

- Who is behind a political campaign and why?
- What methods do campaigns use to get people's attention?
- How does a campaign reach different people?
- How has political campaigning changed over time?

Read on to learn more about the ins and outs of political campaigns.

CONSTANT CONTACT

Political campaigns use many types of media to inform voters. Examples include yard signs, fliers that come in the mail, TV ads, billboards, radio ads, and pamphlets left on your porch by campaign workers. Internet ads, emails, and social media are the newest kinds of media used to spread information about political campaigns.

GETTING ORGANIZED

A political campaign is designed to get people to vote in an **election** or a **referendum**. But who spends their time and money on a political campaign, and why?

Political campaigns help voters learn about candidates running for office. Campaigns help people choose for whom they want to vote in local, state, and national elections. A referendum is a vote to make a change in a law. Referendum campaigns help people understand the issues at stake. Raising the minimum

The main goal of a political campaign is getting people to the polls to vote for their candidate.

wage or raising taxes to build a new school are two examples of issues that can be in a referendum.

Political campaigns are run by campaign committees made up of volunteers or paid staff from a **political party** or a **special interest group**. People in special interest groups feel strongly about an issue or a set of issues. They support the campaigns of candidates who promise to pass or enforce laws that match their goals.

Political campaigns can be very expensive. It takes a lot of money just to get started. Campaigns must train staff and volunteers, print materials, rent office space, and buy supplies. Advertising is another huge expense. The cost of running a TV ad can be hundreds of thousands of dollars. The greater a show's audience, the more it usually costs to run an ad.

A typical campaign has a large staff of paid employees and volunteers. It takes lots of people to phone **constituents**, knock on doors, and create campaign ads. Political parties and special interest

It costs a lot of money to run a political campaign. Running ads on TV eats up a big part of a campaign's media budget.

groups give money to a candidate's campaign committee to cover its costs. Individual citizens donate money to campaigns too.

CASE STUDY
SUPER PACs

In January 2010, the US Supreme Court struck down a rule that banned corporations and labor unions from making "independent expenditures" to influence an election. As a result, corporations and unions could pay for their own TV ads separately from the ads bought by a candidate's official campaign. Two months later, a federal appeals court ruled that no limits could be placed on the amount of money raised or spent by groups that only make such "independent expenditures." These groups, known as super political action committees (or super PACs), cannot contribute money directly to political candidates or parties. However, they can spend as much as they want on their own advertising to influence the outcome of a campaign. Because of these court rulings, corporations can spend much more money to influence federal elections today than they did before 2010.

WINNING YOUR VOTE

Many political races will have multiple candidates. And in most election years there will be many races and issues competing for voters' attention. What techniques do campaigns use to stand out from the crowd?

One method is to focus campaign advertising on "hot-button" issues, such as taxes, war, or immigration. The campaign committees know that many voters feel very strongly about these issues. They try to trigger an emotional response to get people to vote their way. For example, if creating jobs is a key issue in an election, a candidate's campaign could create an ad featuring people who recently lost their jobs. The ad might focus on the hardships that those people and their families have endured. Then the candidate will promise that his or her policies will help those people find new jobs. The emotional appeal is obvious—if you feel bad for the people in the ads, vote for this candidate because he or she will help them.

Often a campaign's staff will research the opponent's strengths and weaknesses. They use this information to create ads and other media that attack

Immigration is one of many "hot-button" issues that political campaigns use to get your attention.

A candidate's campaign team will help manage his or her image and keep the candidate on-message when discussing important issues.

KENNEDY–NIXON DEBATE

In 1960, the presidential **debates** were first shown on TV. Richard M. Nixon and John F. Kennedy ran for president. They had four televised debates. Each man was able to talk easily about current issues like civil rights and exploring outer space. They both had strong ideas and were well-informed. But most people remember how the candidates looked. Some people thought Nixon looked pale, ill, or tired. And some thought Kennedy looked healthy, tan, and athletic. Kennedy won the election. Some people think that the difference in how they looked made an impact on the election results.

opponents. These negative ads are called **mudslinging**. They focus on the opponent's weaknesses or past problems to create negative messages. Mudslinging ads often present one-sided data to hurt the image of the opponent while saying nothing about the candidate whom the ads are designed to support.

An effective campaign will have a media team that serves two purposes. It will help make sure the candidate has a clear, consistent message so voters will

know where the candidate stands on important issues.
The team also will generate opportunities for the
candidate to share that message in the media. An
interview with an influential TV or radio host can go a
long way toward getting the attention of the voters.

*Richard M. Nixon, left, and John F. Kennedy take part
in a televised presidential debate on October 21, 1960.*

Finally, a face-to-face debate can be a good way for candidates to get the attention of voters. Debates allow candidates to show how they are different from the rest of the field. Debates are like conversations among people who discuss and argue about issues and ideas. But people sometimes focus on more than the issues or ideas being discussed. Televised debates allow voters to see how the candidates treat one another. How the candidates look also influences voters. Many votes are won or lost based on how a candidate performs in a debate.

CHAPTER 4

REACHING VOTERS

The winning candidate obviously is the person who gets the most votes, no matter who casts those votes. But campaigns know that people respond to messages differently. How do they target their strategic messages to generate the most votes?

The United States has a two-party political system. The people who belong to a political party generally have similar opinions about important issues. The two main parties are the Democratic and Republican parties. Most national offices are held by a Democrat or a Republican.

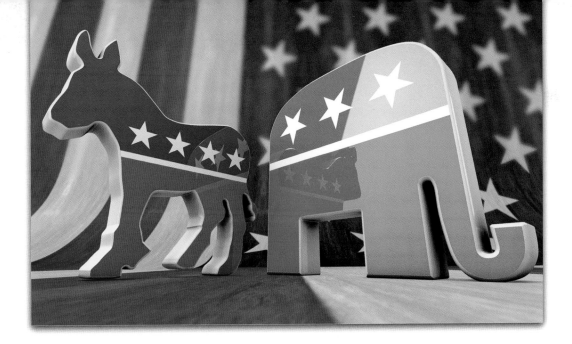

Democrats and Republicans use the donkey and elephant symbols, respectively, to represent their parties.

But many other parties exist, such as the Green Party, the Socialist Party, and the Libertarian Party. Candidates or politicians can also be independent, without a link to a party.

Many voters tend to identify strongly with their preferred party. Those voters are called a party's **base**. A lifelong Democrat might vote for any Democrat on the ballot, regardless of what he or she thought of a candidate's campaign. But most races can't be won by simply appealing to a party's base. Independent voters

and those with less rigid political views—also known as
swing voters—are often the key to winning an
election.

The "Daisy" ad ran only once but it helped
Lyndon B. Johnson win the 1964 presidential election.

[21ST CENTURY SKILLS LIBRARY]

LBJ's "Daisy" Ad

In 1964, President Lyndon B. Johnson ran for re-election against Senator Barry Goldwater. Nuclear war was an issue on everyone's minds. The United States and the Soviet Union had been stockpiling weapons for nearly two decades.

Johnson's campaign committee created the "Daisy" ad. In the ad, a girl counts the petals of a flower as she pulls them off. Her counting is followed by a countdown. When she reaches "one," an explosion and a nuclear mushroom cloud fill the TV screen. Then a narrator says, "These are the stakes: To make a world in which all of God's children can live, or to go into the darkness. We must either love each other, or we must die." The ad was basically telling people to vote for Johnson because they could rely on him to stop nuclear war.

The "Daisy" ad was taken off TV after just one showing because it frightened many people. But it made a big impact on voters. Johnson won that election by a large margin.

When a campaign staff starts creating its media strategy, it researches the eligible voters. The staff wants to know the answers to a number of key questions: What issues are most important in the race? What issues have increased voter turnout in the past? Are the voters more

Political campaigns rely heavily on polls that gather information on how voters feel about key issues.

[21ST CENTURY SKILLS LIBRARY]

conservative or **liberal**? How do voters usually get information about candidates? How many votes are needed to win? Where are the swing voters located?

This information helps the campaign know which voters to target and where to spend the campaign's money. It tells campaign staff what issues to focus on in ads and interviews. It helps the media team understand the voting habits of the people in the area. And it helps the team understand how best to reach the voters it needs on its side to win the election.

CHAPTER 5

CHANGING TACTICS

Today, many TV networks and radio stations are dedicated to talking about politics all year long, not just in election season. But people were interested in politics long before the explosion of mass media. In the past, candidates used debates and newspapers to spread their ideas. Candidates debated one another. People who lived nearby came to listen. Newspapers wrote about the debates for people who lived far away from the debate.

Then radio was invented, and campaigning changed. In the 1920s and 1930s, radio ads were common.

Debates and newspapers were still important. But radio was the new way to reach more people than ever before.

Television introduced a new way to campaign. Candidates could be seen and heard by many people at once. A candidate would buy time for a TV ad. In early

Many current TV networks and radio stations—and their related websites—focus their coverage on politics.

Barack Obama used social media such as Twitter to reach young audiences and help raise money in his presidential campaigns.

ads, a candidate would give a long speech about his or her ideas and plans. Then shorter ads became popular. Candidates realized that it was hard to keep people's attention for long periods of time. Short ads focused on one idea or issue.

Debates were also shown on TV. They were seen as a good way to deliver a campaign message. Candidates wanted people to see them on TV. They wanted people to see them talking about issues with their opponent. They could explain how their ideas were better.

Campaigning changed again in the mid-2000s. The Internet became a favorite place to connect with the public. Now voters can see ads on a smart phone, a tablet, or a computer. Technology allows campaigns to target voters with ads that focus on issues that particularly interest them.

Campaign emails can also be shared by forwarding to family and friends. Newspaper articles, ads, debates and other information on the Internet can be sent anywhere and to anyone by just clicking a mouse. And an email is much more cost-effective than buying an ad.

SOCIAL MEDIA

Social media websites such as Facebook and Twitter made it easier to share campaign information. A candidate's Facebook post or YouTube video can be seen by his or her followers. Those people can share the information with all of their contacts. Those people can also share the information. Before you know it, that candidate's message might have spread from coast to coast or around the world.

Campaign tactics have changed a lot over time. But the goal of these campaigns remains the same—to get their candidates elected. Keep in mind who is behind the campaigns, how they try to reach you, and what impact their messages are designed to have on you. That will help you make informed decisions when it's your turn to cast a vote.

Bill Clinton, shown here playing the saxophone at a political rally, found unique ways to connect with young voters in 1992.

New Media Strategies

Candidates once had a hard time reaching young voters. They were hard to pin down because their media consumption habits tend to change faster than those of older voters. In 1992, Arkansas governor Bill Clinton ran for president. He hired a number of young staffers who were more familiar with the interests of people their age. His media team booked him for a 90-minute show on MTV. The show was called "Choose or Lose: Facing the Future with Bill Clinton." On the show, Clinton answered questions from young people in the audience. His ability to connect with young voters at their level was widely credited with helping him win the election.

Campaign tactics have continued to evolve. In 2008, Barack Obama used social media to engage with young voters. He knew that the Internet was the best way to reach people under the age of 30, a group that often doesn't have a high voter turnout. Social media also made it easy for people to donate to his campaign. This approach appealed to younger voters who grew up with cell phones and computers. The strategy paid off. Exit polls showed that 66 percent of voters under 29 and 69 percent of first-time voters cast their ballots for Obama.

THINK ABOUT IT

When you see a political ad, try to find out who paid for it. What do they have to gain by supporting that candidate?

Think about what impact the ad is trying to have on you. Is it appealing to your emotions? Your intelligence? Both?

Compare how candidates in the same race try to reach different people. Do they use the same tactics?

What role does social media play in an election? Are the candidates trying to connect with young voters at their level?

LEARN MORE

FURTHER READING

Cunningham, Kevin. *How Political Campaigns and Elections Work*. Minneapolis, MN: Abdo Publishing, 2015.

Gerdes, Louise I. *Super PACs*. Detroit, MI: Greenhaven Press, 2014.

McCabe, Matthew. *12 Things to Know about Political Parties*. Mankato, MN: Peterson Publishing Co., 2015.

WEB LINKS

Congress for Kids
congressforkids.net/games/Elections_campaign/2_campaign.htm
Games, quizzes, and fun facts about the federal election process.

PBS Kids: The Democracy Project
pbskids.org/democracy/parents-and-teachers
Learn more about the history of campaigns, voting, and politics.

Rock the Vote
rockthevote.com
Fusing pop culture, music, art, and technology to inspire political activity.

GLOSSARY

base (bayss) voters who identify strongly with one party

candidate (KAN-duh-date) someone who is running in an election

conservative (kuhn-SUR-vuh-tiv) opposed to radical change

constituents (kuhn-STICH-oo-uhnts) voters represented by an elected official

debates (di-BATES) discussions between sides with different views

election (i-LEK-shuhn) the process of voting to choose a person for office

liberal (LIB-ur-uhl) in favor of political change and reform

mudslinging (MUHD-sling-ing) the use of personal attacks or insults in order to undermine an opponent

political party (puh-LIT-ick-uhl PAR-tee) an organized group of people with similar political beliefs who try to win elections

referendum (ref-uh-REN-duhm) a vote by the people on a public measure

special interest group (SPESH-uhl IN-trist groop) a person or group seeking to influence legislative or government policy in order to promote often narrowly defined interests

swing voters (swing VOHT-urz) independent voters and those with less rigid political views

INDEX